PROJECT
Luke

Written by Anne Smith
additional suggestions for activity by Rory Keegan and Rod Symmons

Design by Catherine Jackson
Cover design by Wild Associates

Copyright ©1998 CPAS

Church Pastoral Aid Society
Athena Drive
Tachbrook Park
WARWICK
CV34 6NG
Tel: (01926) 334242

ISBN 1 8976 6096 0

No unauthorized copying. Permission is given to photocopy the 'Group Sheet' handouts for groups whose leader is using the book.

Church Pastoral Aid Society
Registered Charity No 1007820
A company limited by guarantee

CPAS

St Luke's Gospel – Every Picture Tells the Story

God created this earth and all that is within her, and his deep desire is that we, the children of this earth, would come to know him. The Old Testament is a record of the relationship that God formed with Israel, and his attempts to reveal himself to Israel over the centuries through the law, through the prophets and through his actions on her behalf.

God wasn't satisfied. He wanted to give this earth a more complete revelation of himself, and he wanted not just Israel to receive this revelation, but all nations. God, out of his amazing desire to be known by us, became incarnate and lived among us.

Jesus, God's Answer

If we want to know God, we cannot find a better picture than Jesus. In some mysterious way which is beyond our human understanding, Jesus, as well as being fully human, is also fully God. By coming and living among us, God has unveiled more of himself to us than ever before. When we see the mercy of Jesus, we are seeing the mercy of God. When we see the humility of Jesus, we see the humility of God. When we see the power of Jesus, we see the power of God. Jesus is God's invitation to us to know him, to follow him, to serve him and to love him.

Luke's Jesus

Luke wanted to make sure this revelation of God through Jesus was not forgotten. He was not just a man of faith, but a man of science and detail. He wanted those around him to know the facts about Jesus. Therefore, he began to write his account of the life of Jesus Christ.

Imagine condensing your life into twenty-four very short chapters. You would have to be selective and much would be left out. Each of the Gospel writers took a different approach to the selection and editing of their material about Jesus. Therefore, Luke's Gospel is unique, mirroring the special concerns of its author. Through it, we see the facets of Jesus' life and character that seemed particularly significant to Luke.

Luke was most probably a Gentile: in his Gospel, he made a point of showing that Jesus came to bring salvation not just to the Jews, but to the Gentiles as well. Luke was also a doctor (Colossians 4:14), a man of compassion. He emphasized Jesus' concern for the individual, his compassion for the poor, the sick, the outcast, the despised, as well as for his disciples and friends, and for women and children. Luke's Jesus is not just divine but also very approachable, very human. Finally, Luke was a man who had embraced Jesus as his Saviour. Over and again in the Gospel, he confronted his listeners with Jesus Christ. He showed Jesus being accepted by some and rejected by many. When we read his Gospel, we are asked to make our own response.

It is impossible to do justice to the richness of this Gospel in this short series of studies, yet as you work through *Project Luke*, may you find yourself strangely warmed by the Jesus you find here, drawn by this revelation of God in Christ.

Contents

HOW DO I USE THIS BOOK? page 4

HOW DO I PREPARE? page 5

1. CHILDHOOD PHOTOGRAPHS page 6
Luke 1:26-56; 2:1-52
AIM To gain a deeper awareness of the humanity of Jesus and to explore his identity as the Messiah

2. THE BIG-HEARTED WOMAN page 10
Luke 7:36-50
AIM To begin to identify how gratitude and ingratitude, pride and humility, love and indifference shape both the actions of this story and the actions of our lives

3. THE COMMAND TO LOVE page 14
Luke 10:25-42
AIM To consecrate ourselves to loving God and loving our neighbour as the central concern of our lives

4. HYPOCRISY UNVEILED page 18
Luke 11:37-54
AIM To identify the things in us that make us blind and deaf to Jesus

5. LOST AND FOUND page 22
Luke 15:1-32
AIM To participate in the joy of God over his lost children coming home, and to know how much God loves us, searches for us and rejoices over us

6. 'A VERY LITTLE MAN' page 26
Luke 19:1-10
AIM To allow our lives to be radically turned right side up by Jesus

7. GREAT EXPECTATIONS page 30
Luke 19:28-44
AIM To expect to find Christ in the midst of what oppresses us most

8. THE RETURN OF JOY page 34
Luke 24:1-53
AIM To meet and celebrate Jesus Christ, our risen Lord

Alternative GROUP SHEET for Session 1 page 38

BOOKMARKS page 39

How do I Use this Book?

Project Luke contains eight studies which are complete by themselves yet complement each other. Each of the studies contains the sections listed below.

ON THE FIRST TWO PAGES

AIM The intended outcome of the study.

INTRODUCTION A summary of the passage, the themes covered in the study, and some tips for leading it.

NOTES Information and comments on the Bible text that will help you as you prepare. Although you may find it helpful at times to share these with the group, please do so only when needed, not as a matter of course. Allow your group to think and wrestle for themselves when possible.

SUNDAY EXTRA Ways to adapt the themes of the passage to Sunday worship.

THE NEXT PAGE IS THE...

GROUP SHEET Photocopy this for your group members, if possible. (Please see details in the copyright note on the title page.) It has all the basic material for a Bible study on the selected passage and contains:

GETTING STARTED A group builder and discussion starter of a general nature, helping people to share their experiences and to begin thinking about the topic.

GOING DEEPER Questions to help the group explore the meaning of the passage and relate it to their personal lives. Often, these questions build upon each other. Should you choose to skip one, make sure that it is not laying the foundation for the next question.

ON THE OPPOSITE PAGE FOR EASY REFERENCE THERE ARE...

FOOD FOR THOUGHT Questions which dig a little deeper, either into the passage or into applying the passage to our lives. Use these as you see fit, integrating them with the **GROUP SHEET**, working through them separately, or even suggesting one or more for group members to think about at home.

WHERE DO WE GO FROM HERE? Suggestions for practical ways that your group could respond to the study in the days and weeks to come. Your times together will be catalysts for growth, but the real growing will happen as you allow the material to change you while you are apart.

WORSHIP AND PRAYER Suggestions to help your group worship and pray together. All songs listed are found in the combined edition of *Mission Praise*.

How do I Prepare?

1 PREPARE YOURSELF

God is the real leader of your small group. Ask the Holy Spirit for guidance both in your preparation and in your leadership. Relax in him. Pray for your group members as well.

Your main role as group leader is to facilitate discussion and create a safe place for group members to share their lives – it is not to be 'the teacher'. Here are some simple ways to equip you for this role:

Even if the passage is familiar, read it as though for the first time. Write down anything that 'jumps out' at you.

Be guided by the **AIM** and the **INTRODUCTION**. Check for any **Preparation** notes at the end of the Introduction: these will let you know about any materials that you may need to collect in advance of the session.

Next work quickly through the **GROUP SHEET**, as if you were an ordinary group member. Jot down notes, questions and areas to work on. Be honest with yourself, and let God be your teacher.

Finally, read through the passage again, this time with the help of the **NOTES**. If you had trouble with any questions on the **GROUP SHEET**, go back and see if the notes have helped you. The notes are based on the New International Version of the Bible.

2 PLAN YOUR APPROACH

Decide how you are going to tackle the study. Always keep your group members, their unique needs and personalities, in mind as you do this. You will not have time to cover all the material. We have provided more resource material than you will need. You may wish to spend more than one week on a study that is of particular interest to your group.

Decide how you will use the **GROUP SHEET**, and whether or not you will need copies. Select some of the additional **FOOD FOR THOUGHT** questions and activities. Select and plan how you will use the suggestions in **WHERE DO WE GO FROM HERE?** Give careful thought to how you will use the **PRAYER AND WORSHIP** suggestions.

Make sure that you inform absent group members of any changes in dates, times or locations.

These studies are based on eight extracts from the twenty-four chapters of Luke's Gospel. Encourage group members to read as much of Luke as possible while working through this project.

3 ASSESS THE TIMING

We have not put down suggestions for times, since each group will have different priorities. However, we suggest that you write down, as you prepare, your target time for each section.

Try to keep to a basic framework each week and allocate times for prayer, reading, discussion, coffee and so on, even though you may feel that a longer prayer time, for example, is appropriate on some occasions. It is good to end promptly so that those who need to do so can go, leaving others to chat if they wish.

1 PROJECT LUKE

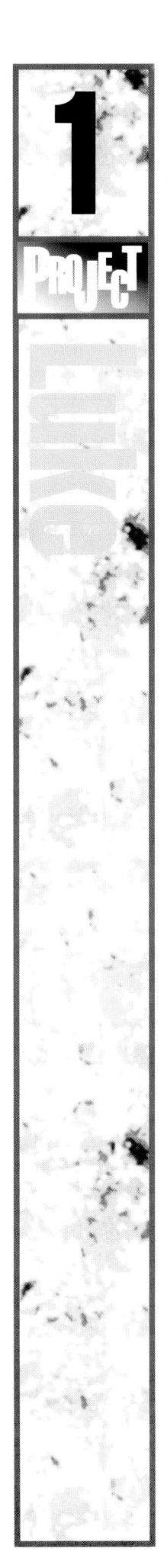

Childhood Photographs

LUKE 1:26-56; 2:1-52

AIM
To gain a deeper awareness of the humanity of Jesus and to explore his identity as the Messiah

INTRODUCTION
Imagine you are looking through a family photo album. What do you see? Pictures of birthday parties, family holidays, picnics in the country? Most families want to record the happy highlights of their history. There were, of course, no cameras in Jesus' day; indeed there were very few books. But there were stories – and these were passed around like pictures to help people remember who they were, where they'd been and what they'd experienced together.

Luke, a master story-teller and the Church's first historian, collected stories about Jesus, gathered additional eye-witness accounts, and scrutinized them for their authenticity. He then wove these stories together in such a way that they gained power, momentum and purpose as his Gospel unfolded. He wanted to confront his hearers with the person of Jesus Christ so that they would have to choose for themselves who he was and how they would respond to him. Luke used these 'snapshot stories' to depict both Jesus' humanity and his divinity. He was not just the Son of God, but a human being with a very humble beginning. He was not just a man, but the Saviour of the world, the subject of old men's prayers and angel's promises.

Preparation Invite each member of your group to bring a childhood photo that also tells something about themselves. Note also that this session offers a choice of Group Sheets. The alternative may be found on page 38. Decide in advance which one you will use.

NOTES
1:3 Theophilus ('friend of God') was a name used among Jews and Greeks. Theophilus' identity is a mystery. It is possible that the name is symbolic, referring to all who are friends of God.

1:5 Herod enforced Roman rule in Israel. Apart from commanding the infant massacre in Bethlehem (Matthew 2:16-18), he killed two brothers-in-law, his wife, two sons, and ordered that on his death citizens be arrested and executed to ensure proper mourning. Execution of Jews was a regular occurrence. This oppression increased Jewish hopes for a messiah.

Zechariah and Elizabeth
1:5 Priests serving in the temple were divided into twenty-four orders. Each order served in the temple twice a year for one week each. Zechariah belonged to the eighth order, or the Abijah.

1:11-12 (see also 2:9-10) Angels in Scripture are a far cry from the Valentine fantasies that we sometimes think of as angels. Often clothed with strength, brilliance and splendour, the unexpected and awe-inspiring messengers of God caused both priests and shepherds alike to tremble.

1:13-17 This promised child would later be known as John the Baptist. He preached to his fellow Jews about the need to repent of their sins before God, and made them aware of their need for a Messiah who could deliver them from their sin.

1:15 John's abstinence from alcohol echoes that of Samson (Judges 13:7). It did not make him holier than other Jews. But along with his peculiar clothes and diet, it symbolized that he was consecrated to God for a unique purpose.

1:17 Elijah was one of the most significant prophets of the Old Testament period (see 1 Kings 17,18,19,21; 2 Kings 1,2). John's ministry would have the same anointing of the Holy Spirit.

1:25 Childlessness was seen as a curse. Elizabeth had been humiliated by her barrenness, but now God would honour her with a child in her old age.

Mary's story

1:27 According to Jewish custom, a girl could be legally betrothed at thirteen, but would not begin normal married life until a year later when she moved into her husband's house. Sexual relations before this point would be considered a breach of custom. While God's miracle honoured Elizabeth before the people, his miracle in Mary could bring her disgrace. Mary courageously chose to accept God's offer. God never coerces. She could have refused.

1:39-43 God gave Mary the comfort and support of two people who believed in her: Joseph, and Elizabeth. With them, she was free of stigma. In their kindness we see the mercy of God.

1:46-55 Mary expressed her wonder and praise in this beautiful song (often called the *Magnificat* after the first word of its Latin version). It powerfully reveals how God works in human history, championing those who are poor, oppressed, humble, and despised. Watch and see Jesus working similarly in the Gospel of Luke, turning things upside down – or right side up.

2:7 Roman rulers were considered gods. But ironically while the world worshipped Caesar, the true King was laid in a feed trough. Only a few shepherds and old people noticed his arrival.

2:8 Shepherds were labelled godless and restricted to the outer courtyard of the temple. God chose these 'sinners' to pass the encouragement of the angel's words to Mary and Joseph.

2:21 Circumcision was a symbol of the covenant between God and Israel, a mark that distinguished Jewish males from Gentiles.

2:22 A month after birth, first-born sons were presented to God in the temple to acknowledge that the child belonged to God, the giver of life. He allowed the parents to 'redeem' or buy back the child by presenting a sacrifice. For forty days after the birth of a son, a mother was ceremonially unclean and barred from the temple. After this period, she went to make an offering so that a priest could declare her clean. Mary and Joseph went to Jerusalem to fulfil these laws.

Twelve years later

2:41 Passover, the most important Jewish feast day, commemorated the night when God spared the first-born sons of Israelite homes whose doorposts had been marked with blood (Exodus 12:21-36).

2:43 People travelled to and from the festivals in Jerusalem in large groups as protection against robbers – women and children in front, the men behind. At twelve, Jesus was almost an adult and could have been in either section. Most likely, Mary and Joseph assumed he was with the other.

2:46 The temple school in Jerusalem was famous throughout Israel and contained the greatest rabbis in the land.

SUNDAY EXTRA

God chose humiliating circumstances for the birth of his Son. If Jesus came to reveal God, then what do these choices tell us about the heart of God? Explore this question by:
1. Highlighting the humiliating circumstances of Jesus' birth, e.g. the potential scandal of Jesus' birth, the homelessness of Mary and Joseph on the night of the birth, the low class of the people who arrived to celebrate the birth.
2. Comparing this to the birth of a member of a royal family, e.g. the fanfare, honour, and visits from VIPs such a child would receive.
3. Exploring what this dichotomy says about God as ruler, e.g. God's disregard for the pomp and circumstance of the mighty, his desire to share in the shame and suffering of the lowly, his choice to be 'Immanuel', God-with-us, rather than merely the God who rules over us.
4. Conclude with the good news, e.g.: that God still wants to share in our suffering, that we need not be ashamed to have him come into our lives no matter how unclean they might be, for God has chosen to be found in such places.

Childhood Photographs

LUKE 1:26-56; 2:1-52

AIM
To gain a deeper awareness of the humanity of Jesus and to explore his identity as the Messiah

GETTING STARTED
There were no cameras in Jesus' day to help people remember, only stories. These stories of Jesus' earliest years are like childhood photographs, giving hints about his identity which would later be more fully revealed. Begin by sharing the childhood photographs you brought, explaining any stories behind the pictures and, if possible, mentioning significant things that the pictures reveal about you.

GOING DEEPER
Divide into smaller groups of two or more individuals, then share the stories below between the groups. If you have a smaller group to begin with, you may opt to leave some stories out.

For each story:
- discuss the question provided
- ask yourselves, 'What is Luke trying to tell us about Jesus through this story?'
- be prepared to share your discoveries with the larger group.

Luke 1:26-38

What different thoughts may have gone through Mary's mind during this conversation?

Luke 1:39-56

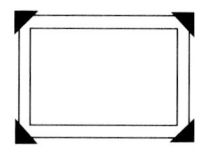

Why is Mary singing, and what does this song mean to her?

Luke 2:1-7

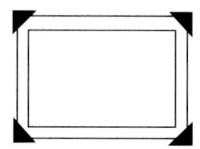

Why did God choose such a humble setting for the birth of Jesus?

Luke 2:21-38

How did Anna and Simeon see what so many missed? What did Simeon's cryptic words to Mary mean?

Luke 2:41-52

Out of all the people in Israel, God lets a bunch of shepherds in on his secret – why?

Luke 2:41-52

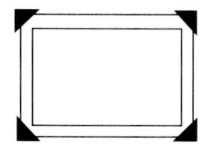

'What surprises you in this story?'

FOOD FOR THOUGHT

1. If you were a Jew living under the oppressive rule of Herod and the Roman Empire, what kind of salvation would you want from a Messiah? What kind of salvation are you, a modern Westerner, hoping for now?

2. When Mary said yes to bearing Jesus, she walked knowingly down a path that would bring her shame and pain as well as joy. What made her say yes? How does this story prepare you for 'bearing' Jesus in your own life?

3. God invites ordinary people to join him in his work. Could God be inviting you to join him in something that he wants to do for your community, church, or world? What are the thoughts and feelings in you as you listen? Upon what will you base your response?

4. How do these stories challenge your view of God or of Jesus?

WHERE DO WE GO FROM HERE?
Taking time out

Mary, Elizabeth, Anna, Simeon, and Joseph were able to recognize and trust God's voice because they spent time with God and knew him intimately. As a group, agree with one another that before your next meeting you will all try to spend a minimum of, say, thirty minutes alone with God when you will reread one of the stories. Invite group members to imagine what it was like to have been one of these people: what might have been the tastes, smells, sights, thoughts, needs and desires that made up your daily life?

Suggest that people make a record of this time: some may wish to write a diary entry; others may write a poem; artistic types may choose to draw or paint a picture or compose some music. Some might even try rewriting the story in a modern-day setting or writing a letter to God. Remember, play and prayer do go together. Let people know that there will be an opportunity at the next session for 'feedback' from these reflective times. But make sure that people realize that they are not being given a homework assignment and that there will be no embarrassing 'compulsory sharing'.

WORSHIP AND PRAYER

Begin by singing 'Born in the Night' (62) and let it shape your prayer time for each other, the world, or those you know who are going through painful experiences. Pray that all those who suffer would find Jesus born in the midst of their dark night. Pray for your small group, that God would deepen the bonds between you. Pray also that God would deepen the bond between you and his Son, and fill you with love for him. You may choose to close with some songs from *Mission Praise* (combined edition).

71	Child in the manger
162	From heaven You came
266	I cannot tell
489	O come and join the dance
490	O come let us adore Him
690	This Child
697	Thou didst leave Thy throne
788	You are beautiful

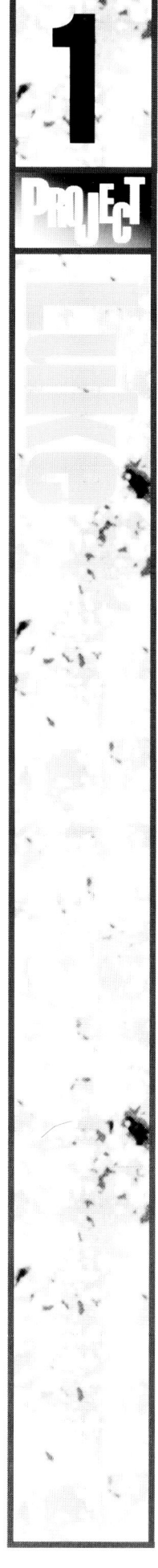

2 The Big-hearted Woman

LUKE 7:36-50

AIM
To begin to identify how gratitude and ingratitude, pride and humility, love and indifference shape both the actions of this story and the actions of our lives

INTRODUCTION
Session 1 revealed the odd birthplace of Jesus, the King of Israel. But if a king is one who serves, protects and delivers his people, then perhaps a stable is just the right place for him to be born, rather than in palatial surroundings. Jesus has a way of turning everything upside down and making it come out right.

In Luke 7:36-50, this 'gospel irony' surfaces again. Simon and his Pharisee friends are truly religious people (see NOTES below). By inviting Jesus, they acknowledge his reputation as a teacher, but they show him little respect, neglecting to show the customary ways of honouring a guest. Quick to notice his faults, they are singularly unimpressed by Jesus.

Unlike the Pharisees, the woman is anything but important, not even to the men who use her if, as seems probable, she was a prostitute. She is anything but righteous, respectable or influential. She is small, despised, broken, and used. But she is singularly moved and impressed by Jesus – and it is this sinful woman that Jesus exalts and the righteous Simon whom he chastises. As Mary sang of God: 'He has scattered those who are proud... but has lifted up the humble' (Luke 1:51-52).

What did Jesus see in her that others could not see? He saw into her inner world. He saw not just her actions, but the motives, thoughts, and feelings that lay behind her actions. He saw that the woman who had lived a sin-filled life was now filled with gratitude, respect, and humility. He saw that Simon who was externally righteous had an inner world crippled by indifference, pride and a judgmental spirit. Jesus responded to them accordingly.

In this session, we will peer behind the story's layers of words and actions in this story into the inner worlds of Simon, Jesus, and the woman. The story itself will guide us as it challenges us to look within ourselves to the mixture of gratitude and ingratitude, humility and pride, love and indifference hidden there.

Jesus is humble and compassionate. He is willing to be born into the lowliest place – a human heart. Once he is within, however, he works to renew the whole person. Where there is sin, he will bring purity. Where there is pride, humility; where there is indifference, love; where there is ingratitude, gratitude, so that what is lowly in us may become exalted. First, however, we must be willing to face what is within us and confess it to Jesus, so that we can again experience the gratitude that follows from being forgiven.

NOTES
In Jesus' day, women were not valued by society. However, Luke repeatedly shows Jesus highly valuing the women he encounters, raising them, as in this passage, from degradation to fellowship.

7:36 The Pharisees were probably the most revered group in Jewish society. In many ways, they deserved this respect. They taught the Old Testament law and scrupulously sought to ensure that their own lives measured up to the law's high standard. They had a significant place in the political power structure of Israel and were committed to preserving the integrity of the Jewish nation. As such, however, Luke portrayed them as the group that scrutinized Jesus most critically and carefully: their knowledge and commitment prevented them from seeing the new work God was doing through Jesus, the Christ.

7:37 'Sinner' may well have been a euphemism for prostitute. She carried an expensive, alabaster jar containing perfume fit for the anointing of a king.

7:38 Jesus, according to custom, was reclining at the table with his feet stretched behind him. Unwilling to disturb Jesus further, the woman was satisfied with anointing his feet rather than his head, a sign of her humility before him.

7:39 Contact between men and women was restricted. To touch or be touched by an unknown woman, particularly a woman of ill-repute, would have been culturally shocking. Simon, deeply disturbed by the encounter, assumed that Jesus would never allow himself to be touched by this woman if he was able to discern her character prophetically. He used this as evidence that Jesus was not a true prophet.

7:40-43 Jesus confronted this hidden judgement of Simon through a simple parable, proving he was indeed a true prophet.. His primary purpose, however, was not to prove his prophetic ability but to highlight the meaning of the woman's behaviour.

7:41 A farm labourer's daily wage would have been roughly one denarius.

7:44-46 Jesus compared the behaviour of Simon and the woman. Simon had withheld from him customary gestures of respect towards guests: washing the feet, anointing the head and the kiss of greeting. The woman fulfilled all of these common gestures with lavish gratitude and love. The reputed sinner recognized something of the true identity of Jesus and gave him a fitting welcome. Simon recognized neither his own uncleanness nor Jesus as a source of forgiveness.

7:47 Jesus explained the cause of the woman's behaviour – gratitude. Notice how her gratitude demanded self-expression. Notice also that she was not forgiven because she had loved, but she loved because she had been forgiven. This leads commentators to suggest the possibility that the woman had had a prior encounter either with Jesus or with John the Baptist.

7:48-50 Those overhearing Jesus' remark believed that God alone bestowed forgiveness. Their response could have been either one of genuine surprise or sarcastic judgement.

SUNDAY EXTRA
Look again at Luke 7:36-50. Now focus on:
- one character from the story (e.g. the sinful woman)
- one action they make (e.g. coming to the dinner party)
- the motive that lay behind that action (e.g. her gratitude)
- the result of that action in the story
- the good news or gospel for this person, whether they chose to respond to it or not.

After exploring these points in a talk, guide people to identify where their lives intersect with the story. Encourage people to ask where this motive is (or is not) at work in them, what actions it produces, and how these actions affect those around them. Remind them that Jesus gives good news to us today, just as he did to the character in this narrative.

Or...
Focus on gratitude as the basis for Christian life, service, and worship. Contrast the deadening effect of a religion based solely on duty and law with the vibrancy of a relationship with God that is based on gratitude. Show how components of a worship service can be expressions of gratitude.

The Big-hearted Woman

LUKE 7:36-50

AIM
To begin to identify how gratitude and ingratitude, pride and humility, love and indifference shape both the actions of this story and the actions of our lives

GETTING STARTED
Describe for the group one person for whom you have felt deep gratitude. What did that person give you? Have you expressed your gratitude to him or her?

GOING DEEPER Read Luke 7:36-50
The chart below will help you to dissect the story and see the multiple layers happening within each character and between each character. Try to be as specific as possible as you fill it out. For example, begin with the **action** 'Simon invites Jesus to dinner'. What do you think was his **motive** for this action? What **effect** might it have had on others?

The woman

ACTIONS	MOTIVES	EFFECT ON OTHERS

Simon

ACTIONS	MOTIVES	EFFECT ON OTHERS

Jesus

ACTIONS	MOTIVES	EFFECT ON OTHERS

What insights or observations struck you as you explored the story? How can you apply these to your own life?

What, for you, does this passage reveal about Jesus?

FOOD FOR THOUGHT

1. In your experience, what parts of your church's life and worship best express a spirit of gratitude? Does a sense of duty ever replace gratitude? In your own Christian journey, how do you express gratitude?

2. The woman's gratitude was so great that it demanded costly expression. Have you any personal experience of seeing this kind of gratitude expressed?

3. While Jesus welcomed the woman, Simon was judgemental. Can you think of practical ways of ensuring that our attitudes towards others are compassionate rather than judgemental?

WHERE DO WE GO FROM HERE?
1. Thanks a million!
As a group, think about practical ways you might wish to express your gratitude to Christ. The following suggestions may help to start your discussion:
- Contact you church leadership team and offer to lead a service on the theme of gratitude.
- Contact a local project for homeless people and find out ways in which your group could support its work – as a 'one-off' activity, or as an ongoing project.
- Identify people who help unobtrusively behind the scenes in your church and make a point of inviting them to be guests at your group's next social event.

2. And thanks to *you*!
How about planning a time for expressing gratitude for the different gifts each member brings to your group? You could do this now or at the end of *Project Luke*, depending on how well your group members know each other. If they share a sense of humour, you might want to include a spoof awards ceremony with certificates of thanks for 'Most Original Questioner', 'Most Diligent Bible Researcher' and so on. Or simply invent a special occasion ('National Gratitude Day'?) and celebrate with cake and thanks to members for what they bring to the group.

WORSHIP AND PRAYER
Give out pencils and paper. Spend some time in quiet, allowing people to read the story silently one more time. Invite people to write a personal prayer of gratitude or a prayer of repentance. Assure them that these will remain private. Move into a time of singing and prayer. If group members are uncomfortable with saying informal prayers, encourage them by inviting each person to express a one-sentence prayer of gratitude. Close with some songs from *Mission Praise* listed below:

30	Alleluia, alleluia, give thanks
31	Amazing grace
59	Blessed assurance
287	I love You Lord
351	It's your blood
366	Jesus is King
382	Jesus take me as I am
582	Rock of ages
633	Thank You Jesus
673	There is a Redeemer
754	When I look into Your holiness

3 PROJECT LUKE

The Command to Love

LUKE 10:25-42

AIM
To consecrate ourselves to loving God and loving our neighbour as the central concern of our lives

INTRODUCTION
To study this passage, some things must be laid on the table from the start.

1. If we do not love we are nothing (1 Corinthians 13:2). While we tend to judge ourselves by our natural abilities or our success at work or at home, our lives will ultimately be measured by the extent to which we have, or have not, loved.
2. We will fail to measure up to God's standard. Our love of God and neighbour will never be enough to earn us a conflict-free home or eternal life. We are sinners, and our ability to love is limited by selfishness, greed and complacency. For this reason, we need a Saviour who can forgive us our wounding failures to love and forgive.
3. When we come to Jesus for forgiveness, he will send us back out to love. As his disciples we are to pursue love with all our heart, soul, strength, and mind as the most important endeavour of our life.
4. We do this not in our own strength out of duty to the law, but in the strength that the Holy Spirit gives us.

This command to love, therefore, with all its implications, takes us not just to the heart of the law but, as we shall see in this passage, to the heart of the gospel of Christ.

Luke 10:25-42 places a famous story between two pieces of vivid narrative. First a lawyer comes to examine Jesus' knowledge of the Jewish law: we are given a clear call to make love our aim. Then comes a parable that illustrates very clearly what Jesus' command to love our neighbour will require from us. Thirdly, Luke tells of Jesus visiting the home of Mary and Martha and provides us with an illustration of what loving God with all our being is like. These elements, although often read and studied separately, are meant to illuminate and balance each other. They give a full picture of the love that must dominate God's kingdom, in which love of God and love of neighbour are inseparable.

Read this passage with a threefold focus. Have your mind tuned towards the passage, your heart listening to God, and your eyes on the way you are living your life.

Preparation Read the GETTING STARTED activity and bring magazines, at least one per person.

NOTES
10:25 A lawyer would have been an expert on Jewish law and the Scriptures.

10:27 The call to love God is found in Deuteronomy 6:4-5. It is part of the *Shema*, a prayer sacred to the Jewish people which they recited daily. The call to love one's neighbour is derived from Leviticus 19:18. The lawyer has joined these two commands together to summarize the entirety of the Old Testament commands.

10:29 In Leviticus 19:18, the command to love one's neighbour was restricted to fellow Jews. In Leviticus 19:34 it was extended to include resident aliens. However, first-century Jews found themselves dominated by alien invaders, the Romans. Did 'neighbour' in such a context mean only Jews, or the 'aliens' over and around them as well? Jesus, in his life and teaching, removed all boundaries from this love of neighbour, demanding that even enemies be shown love.

The parable of the good Samaritan

10:30-37 Jesus used this parable to remove the distinctions that the lawyer sought. He reminded the lawyer that the important question was not who fits the definition of neighbour, but whether he, by his behaviour, would be a true neighbour, showing mercy to anyone in need.

10:30 The seventeen-mile road from Jerusalem to Jericho descends 3,300 feet.

10:31,32 Jesus' listeners would have expected both the priest and the Levite (a temple worker) to have shown mercy to the robbers' victim. The priest, however, may have been on his way to perform some religious duty and would have been afraid that if he touched the apparently dead man he would become 'unclean' and therefore unable to perform the task (see Numbers 19:11).

10:33 It is possible that Jesus' hearers were guessing that the third traveller might be a Jewish layman. Despite the fact that they were racially related and shared some religious beliefs, there was a centuries-old enmity between Jews and Samaritans. Using a traditional enemy as the example of 'neighbour' is meant to shock and challenge.

10:34,35 The Samaritan took complete responsibility for the wounded man's needs. Two denarii would provide basic food and lodging for two weeks.

10:36,37 Notice the shift in the question here: the lawyer has asked Jesus, 'Who *is* my neighbour?', meaning, 'Whom am I required to love in order to fulfil my duty to the law?' Jesus here asks the lawyer, 'Who *was* a neighbour to the thieves' victim?' Do you see the difference? The person who shows mercy to one in need becomes the neighbour, and Jesus calls the lawyer to become a neighbour by doing the same.

Mary and Martha

10:38 Jesus and the disciples were often at the home of Mary and Martha, receiving friendship as well as hospitality from them.

10:39 Mary sat listening at Jesus' feet, the position of a disciple. By listening to Jesus rather than helping Martha, Mary was not fulfilling the role society assigned her as a woman.

10:40 Hospitality has always been very important in Middle Eastern cultures. Martha was busy showing hospitality to Jesus, a highly valued role. Yet she was stressed and resentful of her sister's failure to help. Because of these dynamics in Martha, she was unable to be truly attentive to the privilege of having the Messiah in her midst and loving him in this practical way.

10:42 Because Mary was attentive, she not only gave herself to Jesus, but she also received *him* (his words *and* presence), which he affirmed as the only thing that is truly necessary for life.

SUNDAY EXTRA

We know the command to love God *and* our neighbour. We just don't do it well. Using the title *Time and Attention*, look at one reason for this: our preoccupation with the duties of daily life.

1. Distracted by many things

The Levite and the priest were too concerned about their own safety and ceremonial purity to be drawn aside to attend to the wounded man. Martha was too busy to listen to Jesus or to love Mary by giving her the freedom to sit at Jesus' feet.

2. Attentive to the one necessary thing

The Samaritan allowed himself to be drawn away from his business to attend to the more important need of the wounded man. This was seen as love. Mary allowed herself to be drawn away from the business of showing hospitality to Jesus to the more important need of sitting at his feet and receiving his words and presence. This was seen as love.

3. The choice before us

Will we allow our preoccupation with seemingly important business to blind us to what at times is *most* important, namely the need to give our time and attention, our presence and/or our service, to God and/or to our neighbour?

GROUP SHEET

The Command to Love

LUKE 10:25-42

AIM
To consecrate ourselves to loving God and loving our neighbour as the central concern of our lives

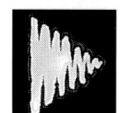

GETTING STARTED
Advertising is powerful. It taps into deep-seated, often unconscious human needs and suggests that the product will fill that need. In pairs, look through magazines and choose one advertisement which illustrates this. Ask yourselves: 'What does this advertisement suggest (or insinuate) you *need* in order to have a good life, and how does the product claim to fill that need?' Share your findings with the larger group.

GOING DEEPER   Read Luke 10:25-42
In the context of these passage, what was the 'one thing needed' from the point of view of the following people and characters?

Luke 10:25-37
- the lawyer
- the wounded man
- the Levite and the priest?
- Jesus

Luke 10:38-42
- Martha
- Mary
- Jesus

Finally, according to the law, what was the one thing needed?

Why do you think Luke places these stories next to each other? What is he trying to say through them?

So why *are* we here?
Prepare a 'mission statement' for your group based on what you have learned from this week's study. A mission statement is a very short summary of intention. Mission statements were developed in business and industry to help employees focus on company aims. They answer basic questions such as 'Why are we here?' Sounds heavy? In that case, try the same activity but call it 'Group Slogan' or 'Us in a Nutshell'.

FOOD FOR THOUGHT

1. What did the good Samaritan and Mary have in common which enabled them to love well?

2. As recorded in this passage, what prevented Martha, the Levite and the priest from loving well?

3. On a scale of 1-10, how busy have you been in the last week? (Let 1 signify 'loose and laid back'; 10 could stand for 'hot and harrassed'.) List five things you consider important which you did not have time for this week. Do you find that sometimes your schedule gets in the way of loving God or showing mercy to your neighbour?

4. Why is it often easier to focus on our to-do lists than to love either God or our neighbour?

5. Mary wasn't *doing* anything *for* Jesus – or was she? How is she a model of love?

6. The lawyer wanted to limit the number of neighbours he was called to love. Jesus refused to play his game. Through the parable Jesus told him to stop asking who was his neighbour and to start *becoming* a neighbour by showing mercy. As a group discuss whether there may be people whom you overlook as if they were someone else's responsibility. What action can you take? If you are concerned about homelessness, you may wish to contact the Churches and Communities Section of Shelter, the long-established housing charity at: Shelter, 88 Old Street, London EC1V 9HU (Tel: 0171 505 2000)

WHERE DO WE GO FROM HERE?
1. Doing what comes naturally?

Some of us are activists by nature and find it easier to show concrete expressions of love to people rather than being attentive and listening in Jesus' presence. For others of us, prayer, reflection, and quiet come readily enough, but it seems risky and difficult to get out there and love the world through action and service. Which comes easier to you? This week, watch for opportunities to express love in the way that comes naturally and take them, but intentionally find at least one opportunity to express love in a way that does not come naturally. As a group decide whether or not you wish to report back to one another on how you get on with this challenge to venture beyond the 'comfort zone'.

2. This is my life...

Based on this study, write a 'mission statement' for your own life. This is definitely a task for group members to complete in the privacy of their own homes. As a group, discuss whether or not you wish to share the results of this activity.

WORSHIP AND PRAYER

Open with singing. If possible, base your prayers on your 'group slogan' or mission statement. Acknowledge your inability to live out this statement in your own strength, and ask for the Holy Spirit to give you all that you need to fulfil it. Follow with prayers of intercession for needs you see around you. Close with singing 'Make me a channel of Your peace'.

1	A new commandment
32	An army of ordinary people
37	As the deer
50	Be still, for the presence of the Lord
133	Father, I place Into Your hands
142	Father, we love You
162	From heaven You came
165	Give me a heart
215	He has showed you
246	How I love You
334	In moments like these
456	Make me a channel of Your peace
624	Take my life

4 PROJECT LUKE

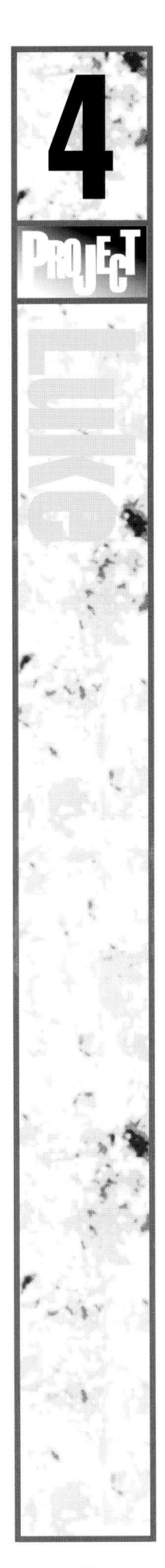

Hypocrisy Unveiled

LUKE 11:37-54

AIM
To identify the things in us that make us blind and deaf to Jesus

INTRODUCTION
The Titanic was the greatest luxury liner ever made. On her maiden voyage, she ploughed through the cold, dark waters of the North Atlantic. The passengers were oblivious to the danger looming ahead of them. The men who ran her wanted to impress the world with her speed. Despite the risk of floating ice, they pushed her through the night at high speed. What pride. What horrible, costly arrogance. Too late, the warning cry came: 'Turn back.' The lumbering ship could not be turned in time. She hit the iceberg, was pierced and went down, taking her shocked guests with her.

Over centuries the Pharisees, lawyers and scribes had built an elaborate tradition around the laws of Moses and the words of the prophets They had created an intricate system of laws to be scrupulously observed. They studied the Scriptures and avoided all they considered physically, morally or ethically unclean. They saw themselves as keepers and defenders of the faith. Yet they, too, were heading for disaster. They had begun to place their trust in their own religious activity and their ability to be good rather than God's mercy. Unaware of their sin, they separated themselves from other Jews whom they considered less righteous. Like the Titanic's passengers, they were unaware of the danger looming ahead. Their spiritual pride would lead them to betray God.

In this passage Jesus speaks harsh words of love and warning to these religious leaders, confronting them with their hidden sin. Unwilling to hear the truth, they grow angry and begin to look for ways to shut him up. What horrible, costly pride. If only they had admitted the truth about themselves, they would have known the joy of being forgiven. Like the big-hearted woman, they would have known the gratitude that comes as a result of being made clean. Instead, they sought to suppress the truth he bore, eventually to the point of plotting his death. In doing so, they would reject the God they so scrupulously tried to serve. How very sad.

This passage is one of several confrontations between Jesus and the Pharisees that Luke includes in his Gospel. It is an indictment of the proud legalism of their religion, but not of the Jewish people, who were loved and set apart by God to bring salvation to the Gentiles. It has much to teach us about the pitfalls of religious life. It illustrates hypocrisy, pride, self-righteousness, hostility, stubbornness, blindness to truth, and other sores that often fester in both individual and church life. 'There, but for the grace of God, will go any of us' ought to be our attitude when we study this text. No church or individual is above this kind of self-deception.

Preparation To help with giving background information, you may wish to make copies of the NOTES for your group members. Be ready to hand them out as you discuss the GROUP SHEET.

NOTES
11:38 Cleanliness was an important spiritual concept for Pharisees. They followed strict rules concerning diet, food preparation and service, and cleansing rituals. Because of this, Pharisees only accepted hospitality from one another, avoiding contact with Gentiles and Jews they considered morally tainted. This led to a strong 'separatism' and explains their astonishment at Jesus' behaviour. It was *not* a matter of personal hygiene.

11:39-52 Jesus contrasts outward 'clean' religiosity with inner uncleanness. Jesus points out that if the inner world is clean, the exterior life will be clean as well.

11:41 The discipline of giving alms is one way of cleansing away greed.

11:42 The Pharisees meticulously tithed a portion of the herbs they used, going beyond what the law required in this trivial area while neglecting the demands of love and social justice.

11:43 To greet someone first rather than to wait to be greeted was a way of showing respect to a superior. Pharisees liked to be greeted first.

11:44 The law said that touching a grave made one unclean. Jesus accuses the Pharisees of being like hidden graves – what looked clean and safe on the surface was defiled underneath, capable of defiling others.

11:46 The laws they created were an intolerable burden to the ordinary people, who were expected to obey them even though their circumstances meant that they were often unable to do so.

11:47-48 The religious leaders of the present were building tombs to honour the prophets who had been murdered by the religious leaders of the past.

11:49-51 The lawyers should have made the words of God's prophets 'live' for the people. Instead they had buried them under a weight of legalism. Jesus is uncompromising in making them aware of God's judgement against them. Abel and Zechariah (2 Chronicles 24:20-21) were the first and last martyrs of the Hebrew Scriptures.

11:52 Through their meticulous study of Scripture, the scribes had the key to knowing God at their disposal. But because of their incorrect interpretations and applications, they failed in their responsibility to the Jewish people, who depended on them for spiritual guidance.

11:53 They responded to these prophetic words of Jesus just as their forefathers responded to the prophets, not with repentance, but with hostility and a desire for revenge.

SUNDAY EXTRA
The following themes could be dealt with in a talk or sermon.
1. Unpack this remark of Scottish religious thinker Thomas Erskine: 'Those who make religion their God will not have God for their religion.' Use this passage to show how depending on traditions and external forms of piety can be dangerous, causing us to miss Christ.
2. Look at examples of religious pride and its destructive power within your tradition's history. Follow with examples of humility and a call to imitate such humility.
3. 'How will you respond when Jesus confronts your sin?' Note the hostile response of the Pharisees when Jesus uncovers their sin. Explore various human responses to having one's faults exposed (e.g. hostility, shifting blame, projection, self-justification). These defence mechanisms shut out the truth and keep us from facing our responsibility. Help people explore which of these they use in relationships, and which of these they would be prone to use with God.

GROUP SHEET

Hypocrisy Unveiled

LUKE 11:37-54

AIM
To identify the things in us that make us blind and deaf to Jesus

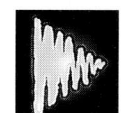

GETTING STARTED
Write the word 'Pride' on the top of a large sheet of paper. Write the word 'Humility' on a second large sheet. Brainstorm, filling up these pages with any words or images that come to mind which relate to these two words.

GOING DEEPER   Read Luke 11:37-54

1. Go through the text verse by verse. Locate each criticism Jesus made against the Pharisees and discuss what you think he was trying to say in each one. Using the diagram below, list these criticized behaviours as an example of the characteristics surrounding the words 'Rejection of Jesus'. List anything else you find in the text that illustrates these characteristics.

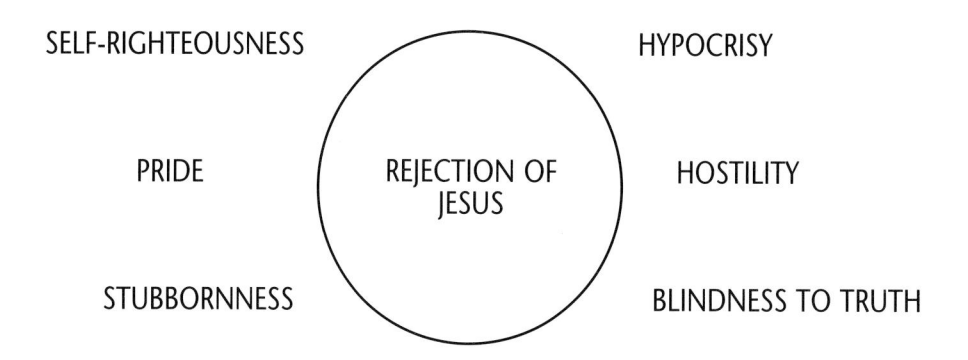

```
    SELF-RIGHTEOUSNESS              HYPOCRISY

       PRIDE        ( REJECTION OF     HOSTILITY
                      JESUS )

    STUBBORNNESS                    BLINDNESS TO TRUTH
```

2. The Pharisees ultimately rejected Jesus, God's fullest revelation of himself and his love. Discuss how each of these characteristics found in the Pharisees and in ourselves may lead us to reject Jesus.

3. Getting closer to home, discuss which, if any, of these characteristics Jesus may be wanting to uncover in you. How do you respond when others try to make you aware of your shortcomings? Can you think of any occasions when a painful experience of being told 'the truth in love' has led to a positive growth in your relationship with God and with others?

FOOD FOR THOUGHT

1. From the best of intentions, the Pharisees offered people ritual, tradition and rules to follow. These may often have made people feel inadequate and failed to help them draw close to God. Churches can easily make the same mistake. Imagine someone searching for God coming to your church. What would their experience be like? Would they encounter rituals, traditions and rules more than God? What practical steps could you take to make your church more 'seeker friendly'?

2. What 'woes' might Jesus say against the Church of today? Make sure you include in your discussion some aspect of church life for which you have responsibility.

3. The Pharisees were proud of their spirituality. They thought themselves very holy. What might this kind of spiritual pride look like in a contemporary Christian?

4. While pride pushes us away from God, humility draws us near him. Look back on the last three sessions for expressions of humility and try to come up with a definition of humility based on them. How can you encourage humility to grow in your life?

WHERE DO WE GO FROM HERE?
1. Great is thy faithfulness
The Pharisees focused on what we do for God, rather than what God does for us. In the coming week, make a conscious effort to remember and celebrate the different ways in which God has been faithful to you in your life.

2. Running repairs
Do you struggle with pride? Find ways of practising some unobtrusive humility this week, such as not defending yourself when criticized, listening first before talking, doing something kind anonymously, or by honouring another person.

Could it be that greed is a 'besetting sin'? Find some simple ways of practising generosity this week, such as giving of your time, your money, your possessions.

If you struggle with perfectionism, try to take a break from striving this week and spend some time meditating on God's love for us in our imperfect state.

WORSHIP AND PRAYER
People are often drawn into legalistic expressions of religion because they don't understand that God loves them in their sinful, broken state. They desperately need to allow God to love them as they are, accepting the healing and forgiveness he has to offer. You may wish to allow space for this kind of encounter with God by meditating on the following image in silence: You are a small bird with a broken wing, sitting cradled and safe in God's hands. Set an alarm so no one has to worry about keeping track of the time. When the alarm sounds, end the meditation by saying these words together: 'My soul finds rest in God alone; my salvation comes from him.' The following songs from *Mission Praise* may be helpful.

170	Give thanks with a grateful heart
230	Here, O my Lord
263	I am weak but Thou art strong
275	I heard the voice of Jesus say
581	River wash over me
583	Safe in the shadow of the Lord
609	Spirit of God
613	Spirit of the living God
627	Teach me to live
635	Thank You Lord

5 Lost and Found

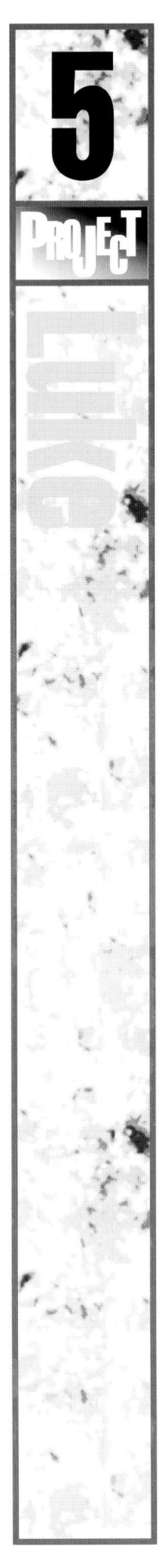

LUKE 15:1-32

AIM
To participate in the joy of God over his lost children coming home, and to know how much God loves us, searches for us and rejoices over us

INTRODUCTION
'The message of Jesus is finely summed up in the saying, "The Son of man is come to seek and to save that which was lost." Luke particularly stresses how this salvation is for all who are poor and needy, and the total impact of the Gospel is to show the "wideness in God's mercy".'
I. Howard Marshall

Maureen works as a nurse in a neonatal unit, caring for babies who are premature or very ill. While Maureen cares for these children, she supports agonized parents as they watch, wait and pray for the time when their babies are well enough to go home. She gets to know them well and celebrates with them on the day a child is discharged. What rejoicing occurs when these children are brought home.

Karen and Peter's child was abducted. Words cannot describe their agony as they ached and grieved for their lost child. Every day, their energy, emotions and prayers were channeled into their search for their child. The child is still missing. What sorrow these parents have known.

When we fear something is lost, we are preoccupied, almost obsessed, with restoring it into our hands. Glasses, car keys, a misplaced wallet, a camera – we hunt for these until we find them. The more we care about something, the greater our preoccupation, the more diligent our search, the greater our relief and joy when we find it.

Luke begins this chapter with religious leaders grumbling at the fact that Jesus chose to keep company with questionable characters and sinners – the very people whom they were particular to avoid.

He continues his narrative with three parables in which Jesus justifies and explains his choice of company. The message is clear: Jesus hangs out with sinners because God is joyful when lost people come home, and those who know God ought to share in his joy.

Jesus used what was familiar to talk about spiritual realities. Pearls, coins, seeds, travelling Samaritans, judges and widows became tools to understanding the kingdom of God, God's love for the lost, the mercy we need to become a good neighbour, and prayer. These three parables are fairly straightforward and easy to understand. However, there is a vast gap between intellectually understanding something and being moved by it. This week, may you be moved by the wideness of God's mercy, his devotion to seeking the lost, and his joy when these, his children, finally come home.

NOTES
15:1 Tax collectors were very unpopular with their fellow Jews for two reasons. First, they were often corrupt, extracting more than Rome required. Secondly, they collected taxes from their fellow Jews on behalf of the Roman Empire. Because of this, they were seen as traitors to their own people.

15:2 The rules of the Pharisees prohibited them from sharing a meal with those considered sinful or unclean. Jesus broke these rules, making sinners his dining companions.

Parable of the lost sheep
15:4-7 Shepherds were held in low regard in Jewish culture. Jesus' choice of this occupation as an illustration of God's love may have been intentionally provocative to contemporary attitudes. Notice that the shepherds' friends are invited to share in his rejoicing.

Parable of the lost coin
15:8-10 Luke complements the first parable about a man with one about a woman. A Palestinian woman would have received ten silver coins as part of her dowry. These coins probably represented her entire fortune. The coin in this parable is dearer to the woman than the sheep was to the shepherd, for it represented one tenth of her life savings. Notice how her neighbours are invited to share in her rejoicing.

Parable of the lost son
15:12 This request, while legal, required the father to cash in part of his property, diminishing both its monetary value and its agricultural yield. The estate would probably have been passed to him by his father and was meant to be passed on as a whole to his own sons, sustaining the life of the whole family for generations.

15:13 The younger son dishonoured his father in three ways: by asking for his inheritance, by leaving home and by squandering his fortune.

15:15 In Jewish culture, pigs were unclean animals. Raising them was prohibited. To Jesus' hearers, their appearance clearly signals the depth of the son's degradation.

15:20 The compassionate father takes the initiative before he even knew what was in his son's heart. His joy outweighed his sense of propriety: a respected landowner would not be seen running.

15:22 The robe, ring and shoes are symbols of reinstatement.

15:23 Meat was only eaten on festival days: the father marks his son's return with a lavish celebration.

15:29-30 The elder son's response shows that it is possible to be lost without having left home: a message directed, in the first place, to the Pharisees and teachers of the law among Jesus' hearers.

15:31-32 The ending is left open. Jesus lets us decide for ourselves whether or not the elder brother will accept his father's gracious invitation.

SUNDAY EXTRA
Many people carry broken or distorted images of God based on their experience of earthly parents or authority figures. Use the message of these three parables as a counterbalance by focusing on:

1. The devotion of God: the depth of God's love for each individual sinner; his willingness to give us our freedom; his refusal to force us to be in relationship with him.
2. The diligence of God: the eagerness with which God searches out sinners, as seen in these parables, but as also seen in the person of Jesus whom God sent to seek and save the lost.
3. The delight of God: the joy and delight in heaven over one person coming home.

Conclude with the invitation to repent and come home to God.

Lost and Found

LUKE 15:1-32

GROUP SHEET

AIM
To participate in the joy of God over his lost children coming home, and to know how much God loves us, searches for us, and rejoices over us

GETTING STARTED
Discuss the following question:

If your house was on fire and you only had time to grab one thing before escaping, what one prized possession would you save?

GOING DEEPER   Read Luke 15:1-32
Go through each parable and identify:

	What was lost?	How was it found?	Responses to it being found
15:1-7			
15:8-10			
15:11-32			

Going further
1. Look at 15:1-2. Why do you think Jesus told these stories?
2. What point do you think Jesus was trying to make in each story?
3. Look at the older brother (15:25-32). What was his complaint against his father?
4. What was the father's response to him?
5. Given the context of these stories, whom do you think the older brother represented?
6. What do these stories reveal for you about Jesus and his ministry?
7. What do they reveal about God?
8. Who do you think Jesus would be hanging around with today?

FOOD FOR THOUGHT

1. Which set of attitudes and behaviours better reflects your own, that of the older brother or that of the younger? Do you strongly identify with one of them, or do you see aspects of yourself in both? What do you think God wants to say to you through the story of the prodigal son?

2. What insight from these three parables surprises you the most?

3. Do you think this insight could alter the way you think or live? If so, how?

4. Do you think this insight has the power to alter the way others think or live, if you shared it? Who would you like to share it with? Do you feel able to do so?

WHERE DO WE GO FROM HERE?
1. Let's celebrate!
Each of these parables ends with an invitation to celebrate. God wants us to join him in celebrating the homecoming of lost sinners. Plan a party as a group, complete with food, music – and what about some singing and dancing as well, if you're up for it? Invite guests. Focus on the theme of 'Homecomings' as part of your celebration. Invite people to share a memory (perhaps backed by a photograph or a treasured object) that recalls a time of reunion or reconciliation. These may come from personal experience with loved ones, or from experiences in the workplace. Remember, though, that the theme may be problematic and painful for some members.

2. Missing persons
Everyone in the group will know people who can be described accurately as lost. They have run from God, or fallen into trouble, or are just carrying on in an unthinking relationship with the world. Think of one person in particular. How can you join Jesus in seeking out this 'lost' one so treasured by God? Pray for this person. Ask God to show you ways in which you can make positive contact with this person.

3. Beginning at home...
Give yourself a personal 'attitude check'. Are there any groups of 'sinners' you shun, judge or consider too unclean to associate with? How would you respond if they came to your church? What practical steps can you take to start building a bridge between yourself and one such person?

WORSHIP AND PRAYER
Give people a chance to talk about their own sense of being lost and their desire to be found by Jesus. This 'lostness' could be the actual reality of someone who has never yet known the forgiveness of God for their sins. Be aware that some members may be experiencing the sense of being 'lost in the maze' that follows bereavement. As a group, pray for one another, communicating your longings and desires to Jesus. Try to include an opportunity for people to repent of any 'judgementalism' towards others. End on the positive note of reconciliation and rejoicing that marks the end all of the parables featured in this session. Suggested songs from *Mission Praise* are:

25	All to Jesus I surrender
56	Bless the Lord, O my soul
181	God forgave my sin
185	God is good
252	How precious, O Lord
336	In my need Jesus found me
351	It's Your blood
376	Jesus put this song into our hearts
445	Lord, the light of Your love
502	Oh let the Son of God enfold you
722	We bring the sacrifice of praise

PROJECT 6 LUKE

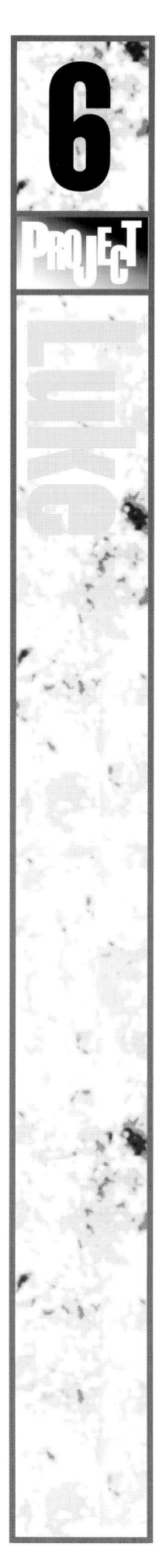

'A Very Little Man'

LUKE 19:1-10

AIM
To allow our lives to be radically turned right side up by Jesus

INTRODUCTION
Perhaps you know the children's song about Zacchaeus:

'Zacchaeus was a very little man, and a very little man was he;
He climbed up into a sycamore tree for the Saviour he wanted to see.'

Zacchaeus *was* a very little man, not just in stature but in status. It wasn't only the religious leaders who despised tax collectors and wondered about Jesus' choice of company. Tax collectors were traitors, collaborating with Rome, the oppressors of the Jewish people. They were allocated the franchise to collect tax from the citizens of a particular area and were allowed by the authorities to keep any excess money that they collected. This earned them the reputation of being thieves among their own people. Most of his contemporaries would have agreed that the word 'lost' was an appropriate description for Zacchaeus.

Jesus' encounter with Zacchaeus is a real-life parable: he searches him out, calls him by name and invites him to a relationship with him. Jesus *is* the good shepherd, seeking the lost.

In the narrative immediately preceding this one (18:35-43), Luke records Jesus healing a man lost in blindness and poverty, and notes that the crowds rejoiced and praised him. In this passage, Jesus is shown healing a man lost in riches and corruption, and the crowd complains that such a man does not deserve attention. Jesus disagrees: Zacchaeus is still a child of Israel and his sins do not erase his sonship, and Jesus here is ready to bring him home.

Zacchaeus responds to Jesus with joy and gratitude. He not only immediately rushes to take Jesus home, but without hesitation promises to dispense of the ill-gained wealth that has caused his bondage, giving half his wealth away to the poor and righting his wrongs. In Zacchaeus' actions, we see the transforming effect of Jesus on a person's life. Zacchaeus responds with his heart, his body, his mind, his strength, his soul, actively expressing his newly born love for God and love for neighbour.

Coming home to Jesus will radically change us. It must. We can't follow Jesus and remain unchanged. The change will be evident in our lifestyle, in the way we use our money, in the way we treat the poor, in the way we conduct our business, in the company we keep, in the way we talk to our children, our friends, our spouses. If we take Jesus into our home, he will turn us upside down and right side up. Zacchaeus, the very little man, has much to teach us about the radical nature of being a follower of Jesus. May you enjoy Zacchaeus, his spontaneity, his joy, his gratitude, his funny mixture of smallness and greatness, as you study this passage together.

Preparation Ask group members to bring a selection of current local and national newspapers so that you can search for examples of questionable standards in public life. What are the modern-day equivalents of the personal ethics of Zacchaeus and his fellow tax collectors in the Middle East of the first century?

NOTES
19:1 Luke has been recording Jesus' journey to Jerusalem, where the climax of his ministry – his betrayal, death, and resurrection – would take place. In this passage, Jesus was nearing his destination: Jericho is approximately seventeen miles from Jerusalem.

19:2 See above and the NOTES for Session 5 for information on tax collectors

19:5 By his actions, Jesus made it clear that Zacchaeus was not an outsider to be ignored but a member of God's people.

19:6 For Zacchaeus, the kingdom of God came near in Jesus, and he grabbed his chance to enter.

19:7 The people who had rejoiced when Jesus healed the blind man (18:43) grumbled at this exchange. They did not approve of Jesus' seeming indifference towards this man's sinful business practices.

19:8 Zacchaeus seemed concerned to clear Jesus' name. He responded to Jesus and to the crowds disapproval by publicly declaring that he would change his lifestyle. Notice that he not only repaid those he had wronged, but he gave half of all that was left to the poor. Luke pays particular attention to issues of wealth and poverty in his Gospel: he emphasizes that the disposal of wealth to benefit the poor is a fitting response to the gospel (see 16:1-31). Zacchaeus' response to the gospel released him from bondage to material possessions. Like the blind man, he was radically and miraculously healed.

19:9 Jesus accepted Zacchaeus' declaration as a sign of repentance and made his own declaration to Zacchaeus.

19:10 Jesus further explained his behaviour towards Zacchaeus using images from Ezekiel 34:12,16. Ezekiel prophesied a day when God himself and David (a figure of speech representing the messiah/king who would save Israel) would come and rescue the scattered sheep of Israel.

SUNDAY EXTRA

Take the statement 'Just say yes!' as the theme for a talk or sermon.

Jesus said 'Yes!' to Zacchaeus by:
- calling him down from the tree
- inviting himself to his home
- affirming he was a son of Abraham despite his sin
- trusting his promise of change as a sign of repentance.

Zacchaeus said 'Yes!' to Jesus by:
- responding with obedience to Jesus
- welcoming Jesus into his home
- giving his wealth away to the poor
- committing himself to right his wrongs and change his lifestyle
- doing all of these things out of gratitude and joy.

In this way, Jesus searches for us. In this way, let us respond to Jesus.

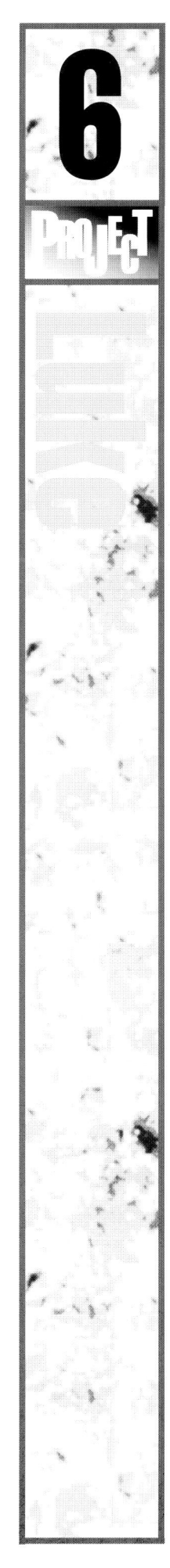

'A Very Little Man'

LUKE 19:1-10

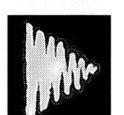

AIM
To allow our lives to be radically turned right side up by Jesus

GETTING STARTED
You will need a selection of recent local and national newspapers. Divide into pairs and spend several minutes searching for news stories which highlight questionable standards in both personal and public ethics. Can you find any modern-day equivalents (or parallels) to the behaviour of Zacchaeus and his fellow tax collectors? Share your findings with the larger group and discuss:

What form of corruption offends you the most?
How would you feel about befriending someone actively involved in such corruption?

GOING DEEPER   Read Luke 19:1-10
Read the passage together and discuss the following questions.

1. How did Jesus affirm Zacchaeus' worth as a person?
2. Put yourself in Zacchaeus' shoes. What were his feelings before, during and after this encounter?
3. Break down and describe the various components of Zacchaeus' responses to Jesus as recorded in 19:6-8. What do you notice? Which do you think are the most significant? Which ones might be easily overlooked?
4. How did the people looking on react to this exchange between Zacchaeus and Jesus?

Going further
Where are you in relation to Jesus right now?
- Searching for him from afar over the heads of the crowd
- Climbing up the sycamore tree in hope of getting a better look
- Hiding in the branches, wanting to see, but not be seen
- Staring Jesus in the eye as he says, 'Hurry down, I'm coming home with you!'
- Rushing down to take Jesus home
- Pledging to change your life for him
- Receiving his words of affirmation that salvation has come to you today?

Where do you want to be? What keeps you from that place?

FOOD FOR THOUGHT

1. Zacchaeus responds to Jesus with instantaneous, joyful obedience. What reactions do you have to the word 'obedience'? Does obedience to Christ have an impact on the whole of our lives – or are some areas 'off limits'? How can we help one another to widen the 'circle of obedience' in our lives?

2. Luke strongly emphasizes the dangers of wealth and the benefits of living simply and sharing with those who are poor. What do you think are some spiritual pitfalls associated with money? What practical steps could you take in working towards a fairer world? For suggestions on how your group could start making a difference in the area of helping to lessen the burden of Third World debt, contact Jubilee 2000 Coalition, PO Box 100, London SE1 0AX (Tel: 0171 401 9999).

3. Zacchaeus' obedience and generosity were expressions of his joy, not just duties to fulfil in order to win God's favour. What was the source of his joy? What is joy? Where do you think it comes from?

4. Read Ezekiel 34, the passage that describes God coming as a shepherd to save the lost. How does this passage, taken alongside Luke 15:1-7, change or add to your concept of God?

WHERE DO WE GO FROM HERE?
Taking stock

Invite group members to spend some time in the week ahead reading and reflecting upon Ezekiel 34. Encourage people to keep a note of any insights they gain.

Encourage group members to do some 'inner housekeeping':
- What wrongs from the past do you need to make amends for in your life?
- Spend some time in prayer, asking for forgiveness for these.
- Are there practical steps you can take to make amends for these things? If so, take them.
- Think of your lifestyle, the way you use your resources. What is one step you can make to live more simply so that you can share more with those who are in need?
- Is there anything else in your life that you know is upside down that you want Jesus to help you make right? Spend time praying about this, listen to what God wants to say to you about this, and follow the guidance he gives you.

WORSHIP AND PRAYER

Invite people to join silently in the following meditation: *Imagine you are Zacchaeus, in whatever stage of the story best fits your life right now. Imagine Jesus coming to you, where you are. What does he say to you? What is your response?* Follow with prayers of commitment, repentance, or gratitude, as the Spirit leads. Take time to pray about the people and situations that came to light in the activity based on current news stories. Suitable songs from *Mission Praise* include:

69	Change my heart, O God
272	I have decided to follow Jesus
351	It's Your blood that cleanses me
376	Jesus put this song into our hearts
463	May the mind of Christ my Saviour
626	Teach me Thy way
630	Tell My people
748	What a wonderful change

Great Expectations

LUKE 19:28-44

AIM
To expect to find Christ in the midst of what oppresses us most

INTRODUCTION
Have you ever been disappointed by God? Have you ever expected God to save your marriage, your child, your job, your savings and felt confused and betrayed when he didn't? Have you ever prayed for something important and watched your prayers bounce back unanswered? Have you ever looked at the evil in the world and said, 'God, why don't you fix it?' Has your disappointment ever led you to turn your back on him? For many, it has. When God has failed to measure up to their expectations, they have turned from him and rejected him as unworthy of their trust.

Perhaps this will help you understand what is about to happen in Jerusalem in the final chapters of Luke. Jerusalem (the name of the city symbolizes the Jewish people) had nurtured a 'great expectation' for centuries: one day God would intervene, and make everything right by sending a messiah descended from King David to free Israel from foreign domination and restore her former glory. He would bring justice, plenty and peace.

Luke shows Jesus' arrived on the doorstep of Jerusalem. His followers are almost wild with excitement. They have experienced his teaching and his miracles. His reputation has spread throughout Israel. It appears that the ancient expectation is about to be fulfilled.

Looking out over Jerusalem (19:41), Jesus knows otherwise. He weeps because he knows that he will not meet her expectations. The peace he offers is not bound up in nationalism and political sovereignty and, thus, he foresees his coming rejection. He also knows that Jerusalem will try to create her definition of peace without him by rising up against Rome. He knows that her attempt will fail, and Rome will destroy her (19:43-44) – hence his cry, 'If you, even you, had only known on this day what would bring you peace…' (19:42).

Jerusalem thought she'd find peace by casting off Roman rule, and all the while Peace was in the midst of her, healing her children. The Pharisees thought they'd find peace by keeping separate from the dirty world, and all the while, Peace was in the midst of them, touching the leper and dining with tax collectors. We often define peace as the absence of what troubles us. Yet true peace has nothing to do with the absence of things, but the presence of Jesus. In the midst of trouble, oppression, unanswered prayers, we turn, and there is Jesus. He is our peace. Can this become our 'great expectation', to believe that we will find Christ and his blessing in the very midst of all that oppresses us most?

How easy it is to reject God for not measuring up to our great expectations. How easy to turn on God when he doesn't remove from our lives the things that seem oppressive to us. But when we do so, we reject the Prince of Peace. His hands are tied, and he stands on our doorstep, weeping.

NOTES
19:28-29 Jesus was nearing the end of his journey towards Jerusalem. The villages of Bethany and Bethphage were a few miles from Jerusalem along the eastern slope of the Mount of Olives. He had just come from Jericho.

Jesus' entry into Jerusalem
19:30-34 See Zechariah 9:9 for a prophecy of the messiah-king coming on a donkey.

19:35-38 The Church celebrates Jesus' entry into Jerusalem on Palm Sunday. The donkey, the coats being laid down, the cries of blessing all alluded to Jesus' identity as the long-awaited King of the Jews. The followers of Jesus were wild with expectancy and joy.

19:38 The people mistakenly assumed Jesus would be a political messiah who would free Israel from Rome and rule over her as King.

19:40 Although Jesus had no intention of erecting a kingdom for himself in Palestine, Jesus was the king who had come to claim the throne of God's kingdom, a kingdom more vast than any of his followers could comprehend. The Messiah *had* arrived on the doorstep of his city, his arrival had cosmic significance for all of creation, and if human voices did not recognize the moment and rejoice, creation's voice would.

19:41-44 Jesus knew that Jerusalem expected a political messiah and would therefore reject him. He foresaw that her inhabitants would attempt to find peace through rebellion against Rome.

19:43-44 Jesus' prophecy was fulfilled when the Jews revolted against Rome in AD 66. Roman troops were sent to crush the rebellion. Soldiers attacked Jerusalem and, unable to enter it, laid siege to the city. In AD 70 the soldiers overcame the weakened defences, broke into the city, burnt it and killed thousands of Jews.

SUNDAY EXTRA
What kind of peace can we expect from our Messiah?
- God doesn't promise a 'Rome-free' life. He does not promise to remove all sources of trouble, sorrow, persecution or oppression from our life.
- God does promise a Christ-filled life. In the midst of this world of trouble and ease, sorrow and joy, persecution and deliverance, oppression and freedom, we will find Christ.
- Peace is not absence of trouble, but the presence of Jesus in the midst of it.

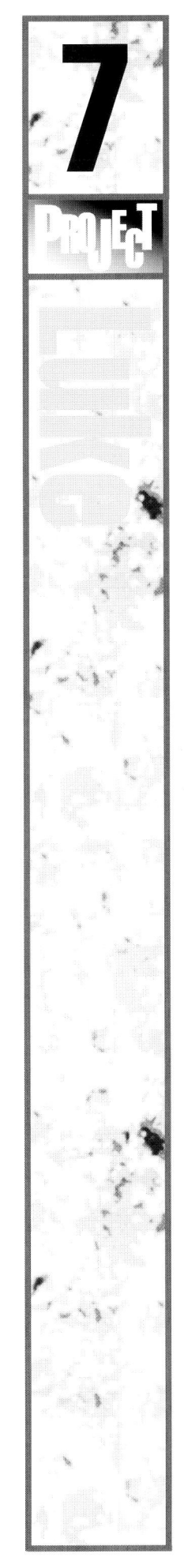

Great Expectations

LUKE 19:28-44

AIM
To expect to find Christ in the midst of what oppresses us most

GETTING STARTED
Choose one of the following discussion starters.
When was the last time you felt disappointed? What were the circumstances?
Have you ever felt let down by God? If so, can you explain the reasons you felt that way?

GOING DEEPER Read Luke 19:28-44
Describe in as much detail as possible the response of the disciples, the Pharisees or Jesus himself to Jesus' entry into Jerusalem, and then explore why they responded in the way they did.

EVENT: Jesus entering Jerusalem

| 19:36-38 | Response of disciples | Reasons for their response |

| 19:39 | Response of the Pharisees | Reasons for their response |

| 19:40-44 | Response of Jesus | Reasons for his response |

Going further
1. Return to the beginning of the story (19:28-34). Luke gives a lot of attention to the finding of the donkey. What was he trying to communicate to his listeners about Jesus? See Zechariah 9:9.
2. What kind of a messiah do you think the people in Jerusalem were expecting?
3. What kind of peace were the people of Jerusalem expecting?
4. Why were they ultimately disappointed with Jesus?
5. Jesus said, 'If you, even you, had only known on this day what would bring you peace…' (19:42). What did he mean by this? What does make for peace?

FOOD FOR THOUGHT

1. Think of an experience of feeling let down by God? What kind of a peace were you expecting from him? What kind of peace do you think God was wanting to give you?

2. What is our society's definition of peace? You may wish to discuss this across a variety of contexts: personal relationships; the work place; the political arena; national and international affairs. What do you need to have peace? How compatible is this with the peace Jesus was referring to in this passage?

3. The people of Israel were looking for a messiah who would rescue them from Roman rule. They were so caught up with this expectation, that they failed to see the true Messiah when he came. Can you think of any 'parallel experiences' in your own life? Have expectations of what God should do, and of how he should behave, ever kept you from realizing 'the time of visitation'?

WHERE DO WE GO FROM HERE?

1. Set free
In prayer this week, 'free' God from the expectation that he should act according to your wishes and desires. Repent of any anger or resentment you have towards him for not acting according to your rules.

2. Travelling companion
Jesus was with Israel in the midst of her oppression by the Romans. He even allowed himself to be subject to this oppression. Begin to cultivate an expectancy to see Christ even in the most oppressive of situations. Try to identify the areas of life that are most difficult for you at the moment. Invite Jesus to show you his presence in these situations – and then watch patiently. When you see signs of his presence with you, make a note of them – and rejoice.

3. Sharing the load
Pray that God will lead you to others who feel that they have been disappointed by him. In what practical ways could you 'be Christ' to a person who is suffering? How could you be a sign to them that God has not forsaken them? Watch and pray for opportunities to speak to them of his love.

WORSHIP AND PRAYER

Now that you have explored this passage and have a clearer understanding of what kind of Messiah Christ was, you can truly celebrate his coming into our midst! You could act out the story of Jesus' triumphant approach to Jerusalem: there is a helpful script on page 178 of *The Dramatised Bible* (Marshall Pickering).

Close with prayer and singing, focusing on praising Jesus Christ, our Messiah-King, who is present in the midst of life with us.

9	All glory, laud and honour
11	All hail King Jesus
99	Come on and celebrate
121	Emmanuel, Emmanuel
242	Hosanna, hosanna
366	Jesus is King
398	King of kings and Lord of Lords
418	Lift up your heads
457	Make way, make way

8 PROJECT LUKE

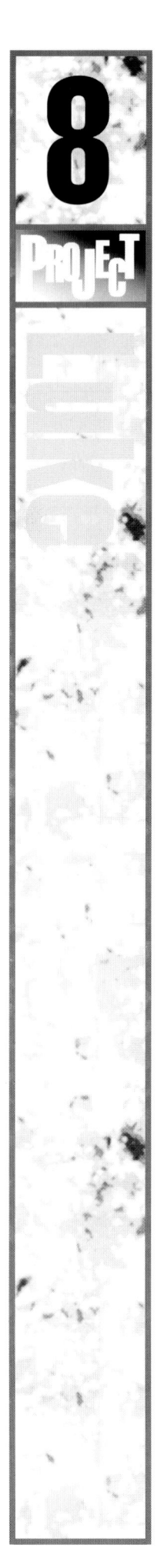

The Return of Joy

LUKE 24:1-53

AIM
To meet and celebrate Jesus Christ, our risen Lord

INTRODUCTION

J.R.R. Tolkein, author of *The Hobbit* and other fairy tales enjoyed by young and old alike, once wrote that at the heart of any true fairy tale there is a sudden turning from sorrow to joy. Just when it appears that the forces of evil are sure to win the day, something unexpected occurs to turn the tide, and good triumphs over evil. He called this sudden turning *eucatastrophe* – a 'good catastrophe'. Tolkein was also a devout Catholic and a follower of Jesus. He said that at the heart of Christianity is eucatastrophe, this sudden turning from sorrow to joy. Christianity has all the wonder, mystery and surprise 'happy ending' of a fairy tale – apart from the fact, of course, that it is historically true.

When Jesus was crucified, his disciples thought that evil had won the day. But what Satan meant for evil, God meant for good. God took the very worst that Evil could come up with, the murder of his Son, and used it to combat the oppression of sin and death. God put all the sins of humanity on the shoulders of his Son and crucified them. When Jesus rose from the dead, the hold of sin and death over this earth was broken. God promises forgiveness and a new life with Christ in his kingdom to anyone who loves and receives his Son. This is the 'eucatastrophe' of the resurrection.

On Easter morning a group of grieving women hauled themselves to the tomb to prepare Jesus for burial. But this Messiah who turned everything upside down and right side up, had one more surprise for them up his sleeve. 'Why do you look for the living among the dead?' the angels asked the quaking women. 'He is not here, but has risen!' From that moment, the world as they knew it had ended, and a new one, a wonderful one which exceeded all their expectations, was beginning to unfold.

Jesus remains our resurrected Lord who encounters us and changes lives dramatically. This week, you will observe the transformation of the disciples as they encounter the risen Christ. As you celebrate his resurrection, may you encounter our risen Lord and find yourself transformed as well.

NOTES

24:1 The women rested on the Sabbath, as Jewish law required, and then went early the next morning to prepare Jesus' body for burial.

24:4 The two men were angels.

24:6-8 The angels reminded the women of Jesus' own words predicting his death. At the time, these words meant little to his followers. They could not conceive of a messiah who would suffer and die. It was not until after his death and resurrection that they began to understand the true nature of his 'messiahship' and the meaning behind his words.

24:9-11 In the Jewish culture, women were held in very low esteem and in the legal system their testimony was regarded as unreliable, yet God chose women as the first to be informed of the resurrection and the first to carry the good news. In view of the improbability of the message and the gender of the messengers, it is not surprising that the disciples failed to believe the story they brought back with them.

24:13 Archaeologists are uncertain as to the exact location of Emmaus.

24:16 Why were they unable to recognize Jesus? Perhaps Jesus looked significantly different, perhaps their inability to see him represents their spiritual blindness. They had not yet seen Jesus clearly, not even before his death.

24:18 Obviously, the death of Jesus had attracted not just the attention of a small band of followers, but all of Jerusalem. Jesus was crucified during the Passover celebration. Many pilgrims would have been in the city to witness the events and carry the news home with them.

24:19-21 The men had hoped Jesus was the messiah who would redeem Israel. Like most Jews, the disciples were waiting for a political and military messiah who would free Israel from Roman rule rather than a suffering messiah who would die to free people from their slavery to sin and death. When he was crucified, they gave up their belief in him as messiah and looked upon him as only a great prophet who had been martyred by their religious leaders.

24:25-27 Jesus reinterpreted scriptures for them, showing how the Old Testament did indeed point to a suffering messiah who would be glorified after he had suffered on behalf of his people. He held them accountable for not knowing this beforehand, just as the angels had held the women accountable for expecting Jesus to be among the dead.

24:39-42 Jesus was not a ghost. He was physically present with them, able to eat with them, touch, and be touched by them.

24:44-46 Again, Jesus enabled them to take a fresh look at both his words and the words of Scripture, showing them that his death and resurrection fulfilled what was written long ago.

24:47 Here Jesus turned their attention from the past to the future. Just as the past writings witnessed to him, so now people must begin to proclaim the forgiveness of sins available because of Jesus' victory on the cross. The proclamation would begin in Jerusalem but would extend into all the world.

24:49 The promise is a reference to the Holy Spirit, who would be given to the Church at Pentecost to empower them to fulfil this mission and to live faithfully to Jesus. This promise is for all followers of Jesus.

24:52 For the first time in his Gospel, Luke portrays Jesus receiving the worship of his people.

SUNDAY EXTRA

A football player won't mature without mastering the basics of the sport. Likewise, a Christian won't mature without the basic tenets of the Christian faith. The suffering, death, and resurrection of Jesus Christ are the basic facts upon which Christianity is built. Using Luke 24:13-35, go back to the basics of Christianity, exploring these questions:

1. Why was it necessary for the Messiah to suffer?
2. Why was it necessary for the Messiah to die?
3. Why was it necessary that the Messiah be raised to glory?
4. What does this mean for us today?

The Return of Joy

LUKE 24:1-53

GROUP SHEET

AIM
To meet and celebrate Jesus Christ, our risen Lord

GETTING STARTED
As a group think about and share real-life experiences of times when you were taken by surprise by something good – for example, by unexpected good news, an unexpected act of kindness, and so on.

GOING DEEPER
In each of the small stories within this passage, a sudden turning occurs in the hearts and minds of Jesus' followers. Divide into three groups to explore Luke 24:1-12; 13-35; 36-47.

- What changes occurred in the people in your story? Focus particularly on changes in the following areas: their emotions; their views of Jesus; their understanding of the significance of the cross.
- What caused these changes?
- What does the story tell you about Jesus?
- What particularly catches your attention in this story?
- What questions does this story raise for you?

Come back and share your findings with the larger group and use key words and phrases to note below the changes you have discussed.

	BEFORE	AFTER
24:1-12		
24:13-35		
24:36-47		

And finally...
Look at Luke 24:48-53. At the end of his Gospel, Luke shows Jesus giving his disciples three gifts: a calling, a promise, and a blessing. Describe these three gifts, and the disciples' response to them.

This is the end of Luke, yet it is only the beginning. Luke also wrote the book of Acts, which tells the story of what the disciples did with these three gifts of Jesus. These gifts are also for you, and as you receive and live them, the story continues. Do you realize these gifts are meant for you? Which one is hardest for you to receive or experience? Why might that be?

FOOD FOR THOUGHT

1. Can you recall any occasions when you have experienced God's blessing in your life? These may include particular experiences of 'calling' or of the movement or influence of the Holy Spirit in your life.

2. The followers of Jesus reacted differently to the news of the resurrection. Some embraced it quickly as true, others denied it and were only convinced slowly, over time. How do you think you might have reacted to the news of Jesus' resurrection?

3. What is the meaning of Jesus' resurrection for you?

4. Why do you think Jesus had to suffer and die?

5. Think back over the sessions of *Project Luke*. Discuss insights you have gained. Have you encountered Jesus as a result of the sessions? How could you share such an encounter with others?

WHERE DO WE GO FROM HERE?
Moving on

Has *Project Luke* caused you to question, think, struggle, hunger or yearn? If it has, that's wonderful. There is so much more that Jesus wishes to reveal to you. Don't stop now! Try to make time to read the whole of Luke's Gospel in the near future – then move on to the sequel, Acts. Ask Jesus to reveal himself to you as you read, and to help you to live out what you are reading in your daily life. May your knowledge and love for him continue to grow (Ephesians 1:16-23).

WORSHIP AND PRAYER

Begin with singing and prayer, focusing on praising Jesus for all that you know him to be. Invite each person to share one thing that they have gained from studying Luke's Gospel as a group experience. What are the most significant things they have learned about Jesus as a result? Have a time of prayer for each other, praying particularly for God's blessing, his power, and a clearer sense of his calling for each member of the group. Close with a final song (perhaps 796), and the blessing found in 2 Corinthians 13:14.

14	All heaven declares
76	Christ the Lord is risen today
155	For this purpose
162	From heaven You came
266	I cannot tell
295	I serve a risen Saviour
478	My song is love unknown
745	Were you there?
755	When I survey
796	You shall go out with joy

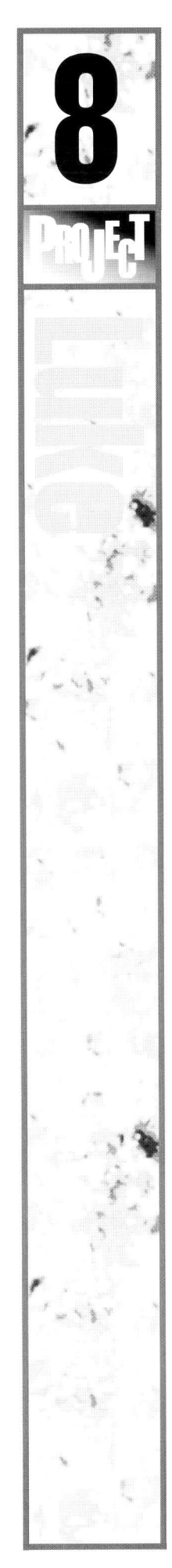

(Alternative group activity for Session 1)

GROUP SHEET
Childhood Photographs
LUKE 1:26-56; 2:1-38, 41-52

AIM
To gain a deeper awareness of the humanity of Jesus and to explore his identity as the Messiah

GETTING STARTED
There were no cameras in Jesus' day to help people remember, only stories. These stories of Jesus' earliest years are like childhood photographs, giving hints about his identity which would later be more fully revealed. Begin group time by sharing the childhood photographs you brought, explaining any story behind the picture and, if possible, one thing that it reveals about you.

GOING DEEPER
Luke 1:26 - 2:7 A humble beginning
- How must Mary and Joseph have felt as she carried this child? How do you think their family and neighbours might have reacted?
- As head of the household, Joseph could have gone and registered in Bethlehem for Mary, yet Joseph brought her along. Why would he do this?
- Why did God arrange Jesus to be born in such humiliating circumstances? What does this tell us about God?
- What clues do the stories in this passage reveal to you about Jesus?

Luke 2:8-52 Hints of glory
- Who are the people in these stories who recognize something unique about Jesus? What drew their attention to him?
- Now list all the people, mentioned or not, who take no notice of Jesus. Brainstorm to come up with this list. Do you notice anything interesting?
- Whom did God directly notify about the birth of his Son? Why did he choose these people?
- Anna and Simeon, unlike the shepherds, recognized Jesus for who he was without any dramatic encounters with angels. Why were they able to see what so many others missed?

What clues do these stories give to the true identity of Jesus?

Bookmarks

We have provided a scripture bookmark for group members to take away at the end of each session of *Project Luke*. Simply photocopy the bookmarks and mount them on pieces of card.

CPAS 1
'He has filled the hungry with good things but has sent the rich away empty.'
(Luke 1:53)

CPAS 2
Jesus said to the woman, 'Your faith has saved you; go in peace.'
(Luke 7:50)

CPAS 3
'...but only one thing is needed. Mary has chosen what is better, and it will not be taken away from her.'
(Luke 10:42)

PROJECT LUKE

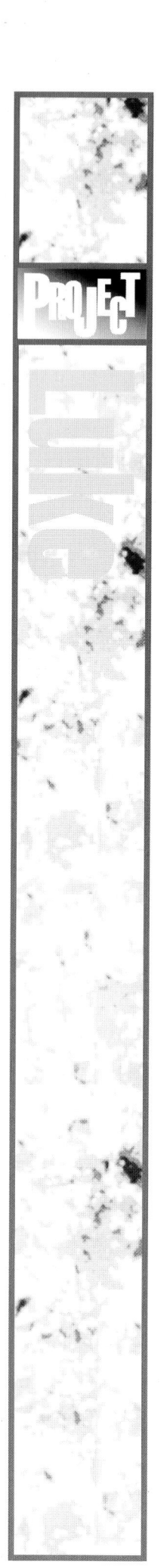

CPAS 4

'No-one lights a lamp and puts it in a place where it will be hidden, or under a bowl. Instead he puts it on its stand, so that those who come in may see the light.'
(Luke 11:33)

CPAS 5

'...we had to celebrate and be glad, because this brother of yours was dead and is alive again; he was lost and is found.'
(Luke 15:32)

CPAS 6

'...the Son of Man came to seek and to save what was lost.'
(Luke 19:10)

CPAS 7

'If you, even you, had only known on this day what would bring you peace...'.
(Luke 19:42)

CPAS 8

As they talked and discussed these things with each other, Jesus himself came up and walked along with them.
(Luke 24:15)